C000088509

inspiration and
motivation for

MUSICIANS

Tamsin King

summersdale

INSPIRATION AND MOTIVATION FOR MUSICIANS

Summersdale Publishers Ltd
46 West Street
Chichester
West Sussex
PO19 1RP
UK

www.summersdale.com

Printed and bound in the Czech Republic

ISBN: 978-1-84953-706-3

Substantial discounts on bulk quantities of Summersdale books are available to corporations, professional associations and other organisations. For details contact Nicky Douglas by telephone: +44 (0) 1243 756902, fax: +44 (0) 1243 786300 or email: nicky@ summersdale.com.

To: ....

From: ....

MUSIC, ONCE ADMITTED TO
THE SOUL, BECOMES A SORT
OF SPIRIT AND NEVER DIES.

EDWARD BULWER-LYTTON

You are the **master** of your achievements.

Truly there would
be reason
to go mad
were it not
for music.

PYOTR ILYICH TCHAIKOVSKY

Emotion can be a source of
inspiration. Write music about
how you respond to certain
events and scenarios. Keep
a journal of how different
scenarios made you feel and
then draw on this when you
come to writing music.

THE DAY YOU OPEN YOUR MIND
TO MUSIC, YOU'RE HALFWAY TO
OPENING YOUR MIND TO LIFE.

PETE TOWNSHEND

Make music a part of your everyday life. You could try:

- writing a new melody or lyrics;
- music practice;
- performing in a show;
- listening to music.

A MUSICIAN'S OR ARTIST'S
RESPONSIBILITY IS A SIMPLE ONE,
AND THAT IS, THROUGH YOUR
MUSIC TO TELL THE TRUTH.

TOM MORELLO

Every musician has a reason for playing – what's yours?

Music should
strike fire
from the heart
of man, and
bring tears
from the eyes
of woman.

LUDWIG VAN BEETHOVEN

Play for an audience as you
would like to be played for.

WHAT WE PLAY

IS LIFE.

LOUIS ARMSTRONG

Don't forget that playing an instrument and singing are both physical activities. To perform well requires a certain level of fitness. Build exercises into your routine as well as things to strengthen your core, particularly if you are a singer. You could try:

- finger, hand and arm exercises;
- breathing techniques;
- yoga.

NEVER UNDERESTIMATE

THE POWER OF PASSION.

EVE SAWYER

Dream the **impossible,** do the **incredible.**

If you're presenting **yourself** with confidence, you can pull off **pretty much** anything.

KATY PERRY

Whilst classical music is
an art form, it is
also at its heart
a form of entertainment.

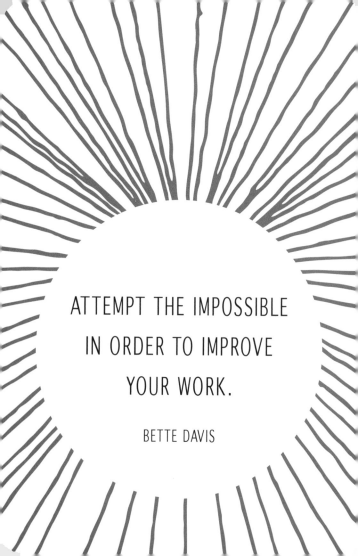

ATTEMPT THE IMPOSSIBLE
IN ORDER TO IMPROVE
YOUR WORK.

BETTE DAVIS

If you are rehearsing
as part of a group then
keep talk to a minimum
as it wastes precious
playing time. If a passage
doesn't go particularly
well then keep playing it
until it does go right.

MAKING THE SIMPLE
COMPLICATED IS COMMONPLACE;
MAKING THE COMPLICATED
SIMPLE, AWESOMELY SIMPLE,
THAT'S CREATIVITY.

CHARLES MINGUS

Creativity

inspires

creativity.

We rely more on
enthusiasm
than actual skill.
Whatever you do,
do it
enthusiastically and
people will
like it more.

CHRIS MARTIN

Don't dwell on mistakes during a performance. As long as you play with intent and passion then your audience either won't notice or won't mind.

TO SEND LIGHT INTO
THE DARKNESS OF MEN'S
HEARTS – SUCH IS THE
DUTY OF THE ARTIST.

ROBERT SCHUMANN

Hook your audience in
the first ten seconds
of a performance.

- Smile and greet them
  warmly and it will
  engage them.
- Start the piece strongly
  to set the mood.
- Play with passion. Do
  you like the piece? What
  does it mean to you?

ONLY THOSE WHO HAVE THE PATIENCE TO DO SIMPLE THINGS PERFECTLY WILL ACQUIRE THE SKILLS TO DO DIFFICULT THINGS EASILY.

FRIEDRICH SCHILLER

No one said it was going to be easy; you'll get there in the end.

One is not
born
a genius, one
becomes
a genius.

SIMONE DE BEAUVOIR

Be direct. If something isn't right during a lesson or rehearsal then address it and work out a solution.

ALL GREAT ACHIEVEMENTS

REQUIRE TIME.

MAYA ANGELOU

Remember the thing that sparked your desire to learn music. Think about it each time you play. Even if you have no intention of practising, take your violin out of its case, stand before the microphone or sit down at the piano and see if you still don't feel like playing.

MUSIC DOESN'T LIE. IF THERE
IS SOMETHING TO BE CHANGED
IN THIS WORLD, THEN IT CAN
ONLY HAPPEN THROUGH MUSIC.

JIMI HENDRIX

Music is everywhere if you just stop and listen.

I take
inspiration
from everything
around me, also
relationships
and friends. And
the inside of my
crazy head.

ELLIE GOULDING

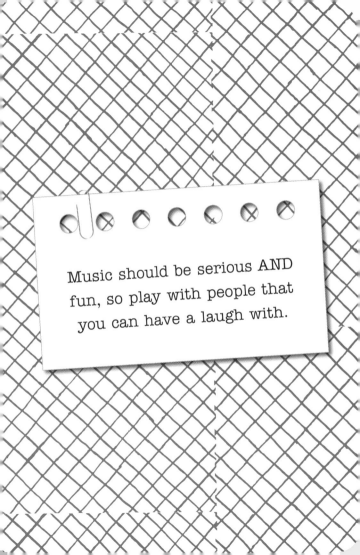

Music should be serious AND fun, so play with people that you can have a laugh with.

A PAINTER PAINTS HIS
PICTURES ON CANVAS. BUT
MUSICIANS PAINT THEIR
PICTURES ON SILENCE.

LEOPOLD STOKOWSKI

Seek inspiration from other art forms. The famous novelist Leo Tolstoy wrote a novella based on Beethoven's 'Kreutzer Sonata'. The novella then in turn inspired René François Xavier Prinet's painting of the same name. You could try:

- composing a piece to accompany your favourite novel;
- turning a poem into a song;
- creating a dramatic soundtrack to a film.

THE WISE MUSICIANS ARE
THOSE WHO PLAY WHAT
THEY CAN MASTER.

DUKE ELLINGTON

We are judged
by what we
finish, not by
what we start.

People often say that **motivation** doesn't last. Well, neither does **bathing** – that's why we recommend it **daily.**

ZIG ZIGLAR

Where possible, have your instrument(s) ready to play. Simply being able to pick something up – rather than spending time setting up – will encourage practice.

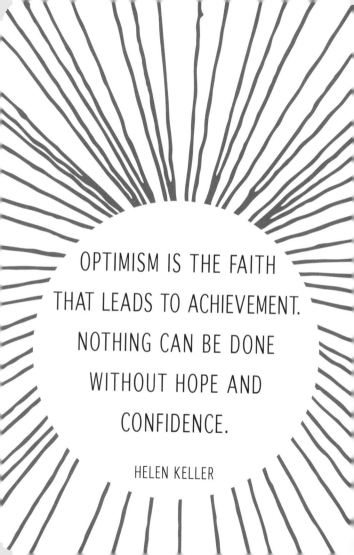

Vocalise your affirmations
to enhance and inspire
creativity. By actively
voicing your feelings on a
subject, you will add drive
and passion. For example:

- 'I am confident in my
  ability as a musician.'
- 'Today I will discover
  something new.'
- 'Every challenge that
  presents itself is an
  opportunity to advance.'

I HATE COMPLACENCY. I PLAY EVERY GIG AS IF IT COULD BE MY LAST, THEN I ENJOY IT MORE THAN EVER.

NIGEL KENNEDY

Make sure that you put **meaning** and **energy** into **everything** that you **practise.**

IT IS NEVER TOO LATE
TO BE WHAT YOU
MIGHT HAVE BEEN.

GEORGE ELIOT

Start with a primary focus. By beginning practice with clear intentions, you can achieve more in a shorter time frame.

ONE MUST APPROACH MUSIC
WITH A SERIOUS RIGOUR AND,
AT THE SAME TIME, WITH A
GREAT, AFFECTIONATE JOY.

NADIA BOULANGER

Listen to as much music
as you can, whether it's
a live performance or a
recording. Pay attention
to what the musicians are
doing by listening actively,
imagining that you are the
one playing the piece.

MUSIC CAN CHANGE THE
WORLD BECAUSE IT CAN
CHANGE PEOPLE.

BONO

Stop and listen
to the world.

Ever tried.
Ever failed.
No matter.
Try again.
Fail again.
Fail better.

SAMUEL BECKETT

Allow yourself to make
mistakes; they will
spark creativity.

FIRST YOU MASTER YOUR
INSTRUMENT, THEN YOU
MASTER THE MUSIC; THEN
YOU FORGET ABOUT ALL
THAT AND JUST PLAY.

CHARLIE PARKER

If you need to freshen
up your love for creating
beautiful sounds, try
playing an instrument that
you've never tried before.
It will either inspire you to
continue with it or restore
your love of your original
chosen instrument.

I WOULD TEACH CHILDREN MUSIC,
PHYSICS AND PHILOSOPHY;
BUT MOST IMPORTANTLY
MUSIC, FOR IN THE PATTERNS
OF MUSIC AND ALL THE ARTS
ARE THE KEYS OF LEARNING.

PLATO

Don't be afraid
to just play.

You can't use up
creativity.
The more you use,
the more
you have.

MAYA ANGELOU

Reinvent a piece that you wouldn't normally play. If you play a classical instrument, try out a piece written for the electric guitar.

I THINK MUSIC IN ITSELF IS HEALING. IT'S AN EXPLOSIVE EXPRESSION OF HUMANITY. IT'S SOMETHING WE ARE ALL TOUCHED BY.

BILLY JOEL

Try not to worry if you
suffer from stage fright.
Many successful musicians
do. It just means that you
care and will probably
give a better performance
than if you approach
it with nonchalance.

IF YOU CAN WALK YOU
CAN DANCE. IF YOU CAN
TALK YOU CAN SING.

ZIMBABWEAN PROVERB

Don't lose **faith** in yourself. When you **feel** like quitting, **think** about why you started **playing** music.

Find out what
your gift
is and
nurture it.

KATY PERRY

Remember to pat yourself
on the back every so
often and acknowledge
when you've done well.

MUSIC IS WHAT FEELINGS
SOUND LIKE.

ANONYMOUS

Work to find your voice. Whether you're just starting out or getting back in the game, don't be afraid to explore sounds. Remember that no one sounds perfect in the beginning.

PEOPLE WANT TO SEE
MUSICIANS SING THINGS
THAT COME FROM THEIR OWN
MIND AND OWN HEART...
RESPONDING TO THE MOMENT.

JOHN MAYER

If you enjoyed playing it, it is not time wasted.

First say to
yourself
what you
would be;
and then
do what you
have to do.

EPICTETUS

Don't let practice become a chore. Set yourself new goals every day and you will start to discover new things with every session.

THE TRUE BEAUTY OF MUSIC
IS THAT IT CONNECTS PEOPLE.
IT CARRIES A MESSAGE,
AND... THE MUSICIANS,
ARE THE MESSENGERS.

ROY AYERS

Confidence helps to dispel the feeling of stress before a performance so psych yourself up by:

- having family and friends give you a pep talk;
- keeping a note of your achievements so that if you feel like you can't perform you will be able to remind yourself that you can;
- reminding yourself what you are trying to achieve.

MUSIC IS ENOUGH FOR A
LIFETIME – BUT A LIFETIME IS
NOT ENOUGH FOR MUSIC.

SERGEI RACHMANINOFF

Discipline is choosing between what you want now and what you want most.

Sometimes you
need to take a
departure
from what you do to
something that's
slightly
different in order
to get inspiration.

TORI AMOS

Use your own experiences
– both good and bad – as
inspiration for your music.

MUSIC CAN BRING A TEAR
TO YOUR EYE. IT CAN MAKE
YOU JUMP OUT OF YOUR
SEAT AND APPLAUD, AND
THAT'S WHY WE'RE HERE.

HAROLD WHEELER

Find ways to relax. It's just as important to build in time to prepare for the pre-show nerves as well as the performance itself. Here are some things you could try:

- compiling a playlist of your favourite music to listen to beforehand;
- yoga or breathing exercises;
- a walk in the fresh air;
- looking at photographs of your favourite moments – whether it's of friends and family, musicians you aspire to be like or from your own past performances.

IN ORDER TO COMPOSE, ALL
YOU NEED TO DO IS REMEMBER
A TUNE THAT NOBODY
ELSE HAS THOUGHT OF.

ROBERT SCHUMANN

Be **patient;** **great** sound will come in **time.**

You may be
disappointed
if you fail, but you
are doomed
if you don't try.

BEVERLY SILLS

Set yourself a goal. Nothing
motivates practice more than
a looming performance.

A COMPOSER... GOES AROUND
FORCING HIS WILL ON
UNSUSPECTING AIR MOLECULES,
OFTEN WITH THE ASSISTANCE
OF UNSUSPECTING MUSICIANS.

FRANK ZAPPA

If you're singing in rehearsal or a lesson and a high note is approaching that you feel you can't reach, don't dwell on that fact as it will cause tension in your voice and body. Instead try these tips:

- Make a punching motion towards the ground with your fist as you sing the high note.
- Reach up towards the sky if you are worried about reaching a low note.

These psychological motions will help you to achieve the notes without reminding you that you find them challenging.

I PAY NO ATTENTION
WHATEVER TO ANYBODY'S
PRAISE OR BLAME. I SIMPLY
FOLLOW MY OWN FEELINGS.

WOLFGANG AMADEUS MOZART

Don't ever think
that you're not
good enough.

Sometimes we have
criticism
that is very
constructive.

CHRIS MARTIN

Try to imitate your favourite performer's style (you can even dress up as them if you wish to!).

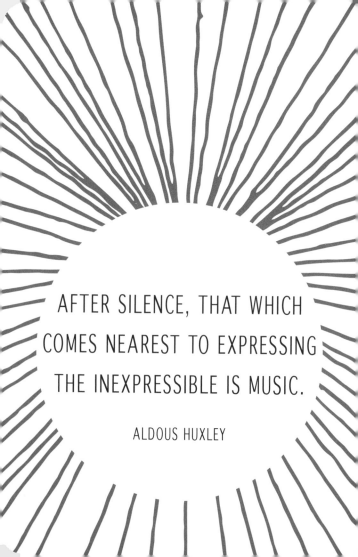

AFTER SILENCE, THAT WHICH
COMES NEAREST TO EXPRESSING
THE INEXPRESSIBLE IS MUSIC.

ALDOUS HUXLEY

In order to project your voice so that the whole audience can hear you, try focusing your attention to the back of the auditorium. Imagine that you're singing to the back row and it will help to carry the sound.

MUSIC IS WHAT LIFE
SOUNDS LIKE.

ERIC OLSON

Think back to when you started and how much you've improved.

I don't try to **sound like** anyone but me any more. If **something** is out of my element, I try to **avoid it.**

NORAH JONES

Don't compare yourself to
other musicians, only you
can make yourself better.

TECHNICALLY, I'M NOT EVEN
A GUITAR PLAYER; ALL I PLAY
IS TRUTH AND EMOTION.

JIMI HENDRIX

Even if you are not
rehearsing, you can practise.
Every time that you
listen to a piece of music,
imagine yourself playing
or singing along to it. Your
muscles will automatically
remember how it feels to
play/sing and this will help
you the next time you do
pick up your instrument.

MUSIC IS THE VOICE THAT TELLS
US THAT THE HUMAN RACE IS
GREATER THAN IT KNOWS.

NAPOLÉON BONAPARTE

Never give up on something you really want.

Music gives a soul to
the universe,
wings to the mind,
flight to the
imagination,
and life to
everything.

PLATO

If the idea of a big performance seems unnerving, then start small by performing one piece for friends and family.

IT ISN'T WHERE YOU CAME FROM, IT'S WHERE YOU'RE GOING THAT COUNTS.

ELLA FITZGERALD

Start practice, an audition or a performance in the right mindset. Listen to a piece that inspires you or that reminds you of how you aspire to play.

MUSIC HELPS YOU FIND THE
TRUTHS YOU MUST BRING INTO
THE REST OF YOUR LIFE.

ALANIS MORISSETTE

Don't **wish** for it. **Work** for it.

Songwriting is a very **mysterious** process. It feels like creating something **from nothing.** It's something I don't feel like I really **control.**

TRACY CHAPMAN

Look for new ways to approach your music tuition, such as taking a class or trying to play a new style.

WHERE WORDS FAIL,

MUSIC SPEAKS.

HANS CHRISTIAN ANDERSEN

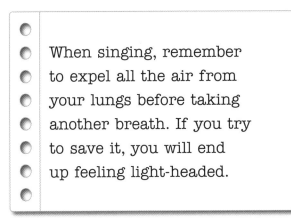

When singing, remember
to expel all the air from
your lungs before taking
another breath. If you try
to save it, you will end
up feeling light-headed.

EVERY TIME I GET UP AND
SING FOR PEOPLE, I GET SUCH
A HIGH. I JUST WANT TO
DO IT AGAIN AND AGAIN.

PIXIE LOTT

Every musician
has a need for
an audience.

No matter who you are,
no matter
what you did, no
matter where you've
come from,
you can always
change, become a
better version
of yourself.

MADONNA

Consider one of your usual practice routines. Could you improve it? If so, then do.

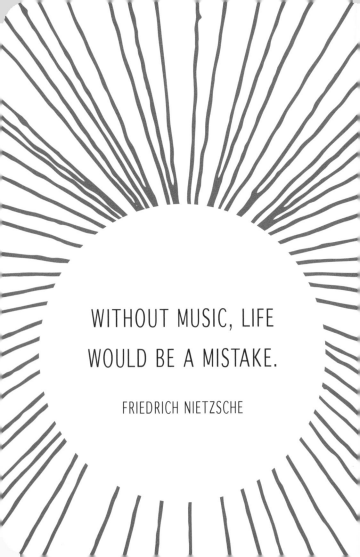

WITHOUT MUSIC, LIFE
WOULD BE A MISTAKE.

FRIEDRICH NIETZSCHE

Rehearse with a metronome. It may seem boring but timing is a key aspect of great musicality. It will impact your ability to perform as a group or with accompaniment.

WHEN THINGS GO WRONG,

DON'T GO WITH THEM.

ELVIS PRESLEY

Push yourself
a bit harder.

Music is
forever;
music should
grow
and mature with you.

PAUL SIMON

Try putting words to instrumental melodies, to help with the phrasing. It could be a short sentence repeated over and over, or a shopping list!

MUSIC COMES FROM A
PLACE WE DON'T KNOW.

CHRIS MARTIN

When singing, it is important that you maintain a good posture. Imagine that you have a string attached at the top of your head to the ceiling. It will create an upright but relaxed stance.

EVERY ARTIST WAS

FIRST AN AMATEUR.

RALPH WALDO EMERSON

If you don't
give up today,
tomorrow you
will do better.

Don't over-rehearse. If there are fewer opportunities to sharpen your piece then each session will be more focused.

MUSICIANS DON'T RETIRE;
THEY STOP WHEN THERE'S
NO MORE MUSIC IN THEM.

LOUIS ARMSTRONG

If you're interested in finding
out more about our books, find
us on Facebook at Summersdale
Publishers and follow us on
Twitter at @Summersdale.

WWW.SUMMERSDALE.COM